THEN & NOW

CUMBERLAND

OPPOSITE: This early postcard view of Cumberland looks across the city towards the Narrows, a natural passage to the west. (Courtesy of the author.)

THEN & NOW

CUMBERLAND

Patrick H. Stakem

Library of Congress Control Number: 2010931331

Published by Arcadia Publishing
Charleston, South Carolina

Printed in the United States of America

For all general information, please contact Arcadia Publishing:
Telephone 843-853-2070
Fax 843-853-0044
E-mail sales@arcadiapublishing.com
For customer service and orders:
Toll-Free 1-888-313-2665

Visit us on the Internet at www.arcadiapublishing.com

ON THE COVER: Looking east from Wills Creek, the images on the front cover show Baltimore Street. The downtown area has changed greatly and is now closed to traffic. (Then image, courtesy of the A. Feldstein collection; now image, courtesy of John A. Bone.)

ON THE BACK COVER: This view down Baltimore Street, looking west from Mechanic Street, shows the Emmanuel Episcopal Church. The horse and wagon date the picture to the beginning of the 20th century. The West Virginia Central Railway Station is to the left, and the iron bridge over Wills Creek is due to be replaced with a more modern structure. (Courtesy of the A. Feldstein collection.)

CONTENTS

ACKNOWLEDGMENTS

The work of many is gathered together in this book. Organizations such as the Western Maryland Chapter of the National Railway Historical Society, the Preservation Society of Allegany County, and the Allegany County Library System assisted in this effort.

Without the generosity of Al Feldstein in loaning many images from his historical postcard collection, this book could not have been done. Special thanks to Dan Whetzel and the Allegany County Board of Education, as well as Mike McKenzie. Professional photographer John A. Bone contributed expertise and contemporary photographs. My wife, Nancy, helped with the editing and photograph expeditions, and my daughter, Mercedes, contributed some of the contemporary pictures. My good friend Ray Lloyd also helped on the photograph shoots.

Unless otherwise stated, I photographed the contemporary pictures.

INTRODUCTION

In the early 1700s, if you traveled by horseback up the Potomac River from Tidewater, you would reach the confluence of Wills Creek in a few days. To the west, Wills Creek emerged from an impressive canyon, now called the Narrows. There was a small Native American settlement, which is where the Ohio Company later built a small blockhouse and trading center. The lands either belonged to Lord Fairfax of Virginia or to Cecil Calvert of Maryland; no one had yet done the survey. More importantly, the area was on the westernmost border of the British Empire in North America with New France. A world war, of which the French and Indian War was a part, would later be fought here. The native people would fight on both sides of the conflict and, in the end, be the losers.

Fort Cumberland, built by Virginia Militia and named for a famous British general (and son of the King George II), would be the first major construction in the area. General Braddock led his expedition against the French at Fort Duquesne from here, but it didn't turn out well. After the French and Indian War and the American Revolution, President Washington returned to the fort to review the troops in the Whiskey Rebellion incident. By this time, a small frontier settlement had built up along the river and the creek.

Cumberland is a transportation nexus. The National Road heads west from there. The Baltimore and Ohio Railroad (B&O) and the Chesapeake and Ohio (C&O) Canal raced to Cumberland on their ways west to the Ohio River. The second airport in the nation was built there, halfway between the Wright brothers' factory and the first airport in College Park, Maryland.

In the 19th century, industry was based on coal, and the economy boomed. No major action took place during the Civil War, sparing the area the ravages of war. A bored Union general, in encampment, found time to pen the novel *Ben Hur*. Two Union generals, hurried from their beds in a local downtown hotel by Confederate raiders, found themselves in Richmond. Cumberland was a border town, with supporters of both the North and the South.

After the war, the industrial revolution took over as major and minor industries sprang up. These included glass factories, railroad shops, canal boatyards, iron foundries, and their supporting industries. The homes of the rich and famous lined fashionable Washington Street. After World War I, a major textile plant and a tire factory were built. The economy went into overdrive for World War II.

Then a slow decline began in the 1960s and 1970s. A glass factory was built, but it was not an overwhelming success. Many buildings were abandoned. An urban renewal program with federal funding was started. Many buildings were razed, and downtown was revitalized as a pedestrian mall, with an interstate that was built through the heart of the city. But prosperity was a long time in coming back.

Now marketing itself as a haven for arts and crafts and a tourist destination for the Baltimore-Washington area and Pittsburgh, Cumberland is on the rebound. The smokestacks are gone, and the tourists come in droves. Some stay, savoring the slow pace, clean air, and friendly people.

Several major projects have changed Cumberland. The construction of the fort was the first, followed by the National Road. The arrival of the Baltimore and Ohio Railroad and the Chesapeake and Ohio Canal were very significant. The flood-control system, completed in the 1960s, was an important event. Both the participation in urban renewal and the placement of Interstate 68 on a raised bridge changed the landscape of downtown Cumberland.

Built along Wills Creek and the Potomac River, Cumberland is mostly surrounded by mountains. Scenic views are everywhere. The downtown-area mall is a vibrant place, with frequent music concerts, the farmers market, and other community activities. Large and medium industry is mostly gone, but a multitude of smaller businesses have evolved, and access to high-speed digital communications helps the technology-based businesses. A countywide bus system handles the needs of citizens without cars, and the Cumberland Airport, located in West Virginia, links with Baltimore and Pittsburgh. North-south corridors Interstate 219 and Interstate 220 cross the major east-west Interstate 68. Cumberland is the seat of Allegany County, so state, county, federal, and local agencies have offices and facilities there. There is an excellent school system for primary and secondary education, vocational training, and a community college.

Much has been lost, but a lot has been gained. Quiet, tree-lined streets would be recognizable to those from 100 years past. The Great Allegheny Passage goes through town, allowing for bikers or hikers to travel between Pittsburgh and Washington, D.C. The steam-powered excursion train of the Western Maryland Scenic Railroad draws enthusiasts from a wide region. Part of the canal has been refilled with water. There is talk of once again allowing recreational boating on the Potomac.

This book will show some of the changes that have occurred in Cumberland over the years, which have either preserved objects from the past or replaced them.

CHAPTER

1

VIEWS

This skyline view of Cumberland, looking from the south and across the Potomac River in Ridgeley, West Virginia, shows the iconic courthouse and the church steeples. At this time, the Potomac was still used for recreational boating. Frequent flooding of downtown would eventually result in the construction of levees and channels to direct floodwater. (Courtesy of the author.)

A view of Cumberland from nearby Ridgeley, West Virginia, shows the bridge across the Potomac River. The Allegany County Courthouse and several church steeples are visible in the skyline. That bridge has since been replaced by the newer "Blue Bridge" at a slightly different alignment, but the view is essentially unchanged. (Then image, courtesy of the author.)

Here is the new Blue Bridge between Cumberland and Ridgeley. The old bridge's original blue color faded over time, exposing its aluminum paint; however, the name "Blue Bridge" stuck, which people found confusing. This new bridge connecting Cumberland and Ridgeley was painted blue, just like the first bridge. Note how the old and new bridges are visible in the photograph above. (Then image, courtesy of the M. McKenzie collection.)

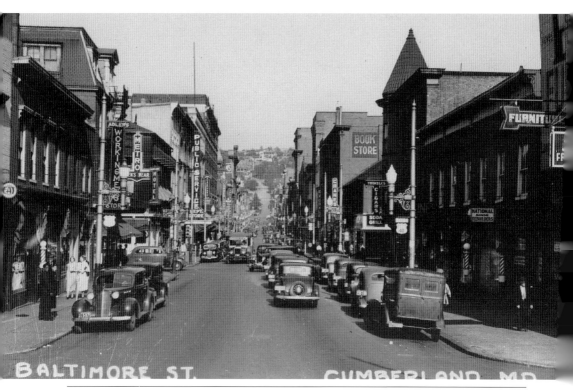

Baltimore Street looking east from Mechanic shows a vastly different view from the 1930s to the present. Then, the downtown had traffic congestion and parking issues. Now, it is reserved as a pedestrian mall. Most of the buildings are the same, but only a few original businesses remain. (Then image, courtesy of the M. McKenzie collection.)

There is ice on the Potomac River, and the residents of the city are taking advantage of this to engage in skating. The river no longer freezes over, less due to global warming than to rechanneling the river for flood control. If the river ever freezes again, it would be possible to skate to West Virginia. (Then image, courtesy of the M. McKenzie collection.)

Opened in 1899, the Wills Mountain Inn is perched on the top of Wills Mountain. At different times, it was a sanatorium and a popular resort. Unfortunately, the building burned in 1931. The Artmor Plastics Factory was built near the site in 1946. It remains in business today, producing plastic bowls and other household items. (Then image, courtesy of the author.)

Campo Bello, a Union Civil War encampment of an Illinois outfit commanded by Lew Wallace, was located where the athletic field of Allegany High School is today. This outfit did not see much action, which gave Wallace time to write his novel *Ben Hur*. The site had been a Shawnee Indian camp. Allegany High School was built in 1926 and is still in service. (Then image, courtesy of the A. Feldstein collection.)

George Washington's log cabin that he used as an office during his time at Fort Cumberland is now located in Riverside Park. As a Virginia Militia officer, he accompanied General Braddock to Fort Duquesne and then brought the survivors back to the fort. He last visited the location in 1794, when he led federal troops against the "Whiskey Rebels" of Western Pennsylvania. (Then image, courtesy of the A. Feldstein collection.)

CHAPTER

DOWNTOWN

The Cumberland Cloak and Suit Store is being decorated for the Christmas season in the 1950s. Shopping on Baltimore Street for the holidays was a major event then. (Courtesy of the A. Feldstein collection.)

The Barnum House was constructed in 1845 on the corner of George and Baltimore Streets. A historical marker commemorates where two Union generals were kidnapped from the Barnum and the nearby Revere House by Confederate rangers in 1865. At the time of the generals' kidnappings, two other Union officers who went on to become Presidents McKinley and Hayes were also in these buildings. The building was remodeled into the Windsor Hotel in 1884 and was later demolished in 1959. It is now the site of Liberty Trust Bank. (Then image, courtesy of the A. Feldstein collection.)

THE ALGONQUIN HOTEL
H. Frank Osborn, Manager
Cumberland. Maryland

Architect W. F. Frederick of Washington, D.C., designed the Algonquin Hotel. It opened in 1926 as an apartment hotel and was remodeled into a commercial hotel in 1936. It had 125 rooms on six floors, with two elevators. The basement was an underground parking garage. It stood vacant in 1986 but was remodeled and converted to an assisted living community. It reopened in 1989 and operates as the Kensington-Algonquin. The building is on the National Register of Historic Places. (Then image, courtesy of the A. Feldstein collection.)

The Fort Cumberland Hotel is located at the corner of Baltimore and Liberty Streets. The substantial, six-story brick structure was built in 1917. It was a typical small city hotel, serving the business traveler arriving on the Baltimore and Ohio Railroad. It had 170 guest rooms. It hosted several commercial enterprises at street level. The building now serves as the Cumberland Arms, apartments for seniors. (Then image, courtesy of the A. Feldstein collection.)

DOWNTOWN

The Brunswick Hotel is located at the east end of Baltimore Street, along the Baltimore and Ohio tracks. The steam locomotive is Baltimore and Ohio's No. 6007, a Big Six built by the Baldwin Locomotive Works in 1914. In the modern view, CSX diesel locomotive No. 5462 is a General Electric ES44DC model. Both locomotives await their assault on the Sand Patch Grade on the way to Pittsburgh. The building is now used as a liquor store. (Then image, courtesy of the Dan Whetzel collection; now image courtesy of John A. Bone.)

Originally named the Sterling Hotel, this property survived into the 21st century. It became the York Hotel on Maryland Avenue. On the left, Cumberland and Pennsylvania Railroad locomotive No. 18, built at the Mount Savage Shops in 1896, is visible. Today CSX's Sand Patch Grade helper engines park at the same spot. Note the parade coming across the tracks in the older photograph. The site is now a vacant lot. (Then image, courtesy of the Al Feldstein collection.)

This Cumberland downtown view is looking east along Baltimore Street, which is the commercial and banking center of the city. Mechanic Street, located east of Wills Creek and perpendicular to Baltimore Street, was the artisans' center. It was served by a millstream that emptied into Wills Creek. The Baltimore and Ohio Railroad tracks mark the eastern boundary of Baltimore Street. (Then image, courtesy of the A. Feldstein collection, now image courtesy of Cumberland photographer H. W. Brooks.)

This Cumberland downtown view is looking west along Baltimore Street. The Emmanuel Episcopal Church, built on the original site of Fort Cumberland, dominates the view. Baltimore Street extends to the Western Maryland Railway tracks and Wills Creek. In order from west to east, Mechanic, Liberty, Centre, and George Streets cross it. The Downtown Cumberland Historic District includes 107 buildings. (Then image, courtesy of the A. Feldstein collection.)

In 1889, the Rosenbaum Department Store was built at 118 Baltimore Street and featured an electric elevator, the first in the area. Local George Seibert was the architect. The department store firm was founded in 1849 by the Rosenbaum brothers and operated until 1973. The building now houses the M&T Bank. Large department stores have mostly gone by the wayside in downtown America. (Then image, courtesy of the A. Feldstein collection.)

At the east end of Baltimore Street, the main YMCA was located on a triangular lot. Built in 1925, the three-story brick building included an indoor swimming pool as well as pool rooms, a gymnasium, a cafeteria, and 71 dorm rooms. It is listed on the National Register of Historic Places. It is still in use as a sports and community center. (Then image, courtesy of the A. Feldstein collection.)

The original YMCA was located on Baltimore Street. It is a Wright Butler design of 1911. When the new YMCA building was constructed at the east end of town in 1926, the old one became the Schwarzenbach Brothers Department Store. The Peskins Shoe Store occupied it at one time. The YMCA sign is still visible at the top of the building. The third floor was added in 1910. The building now houses art displays. (Then image, courtesy of the A. Feldstein collection.)

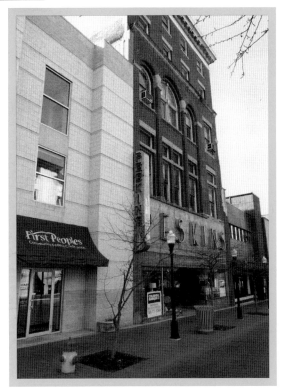

The McMullen Building on Baltimore Street housed the McMullen Brothers Department Store. It was originally faced in white, enameled brick that was manufactured in Mount Savage. The site was later occupied by the G. C. Murphy's 5¢ and 10¢ store and featured the first escalators in town. A victim of changing trends in retail, the building is vacant, awaiting reuse. (Then image, courtesy of the A. Feldstein collection.)

The Metro Clothes store provided garments for the workingman for many years in downtown Cumberland. It was located at the southwest corner of Baltimore and Mechanic Streets, tucked away in a niche of the current Times-News Building. The site is now a pleasant park, offering a quiet refuge for those living downtown. (Then image, courtesy of the A. Feldstein collection.)

This view of the Baltimore Street Bridge was taken looking south across the Western Maryland Railway Bridge. The bridge is an iron truss design. There are canal boats in Wills Creek. No canal boats are in the modern view, and the railroad bridge has been strengthened to handle heavy freight. All the rails that can be seen now are part of the daily tourist excursions to Frostburg. (Then image, courtesy of the M. McKenzie collection.)

CHAPTER 3

INDUSTRY

Cumberland was a center of industry, with two major breweries, many glass plants, a tire factory, textile manufactories, a world-class fabric cleaning establishment, a steel products manufactory, and many small supporting industries. The boats for the C&O Canal were built here. (Courtesy of the A. Feldstein collection.)

The Celanese Fibers Plant was built during World War I to produce acetate dope for aircraft fabric. The location was chosen to provide protection against zeppelin attacks. The plant was not completed before the war's end, and production was shifted to acetate yarn, first produced in 1924. It was billed as "artificial silk." The plant closed in the 1980s, and the site now houses state and federal prisons. (Then image, courtesy of the A. Feldstein collection.)

The Footer Dye Works, founded in 1870 by Thomas Footer, was located at South Mechanic and Liberty Streets in 1904. They once had over 500 employees, with branch offices in 20 cities. Even the White House shipped cleaning to this facility. It closed in 1937, and the big building became the Tri-State Mine and Mill Supply. It is now vacant and looking for reuse. The adjacent Footer-owned Sawtooth Building, so named because its roof allowed for natural lighting, was torn down in 2009. (Then image, courtesy of the A. Feldstein collection.)

The Silk Mill Building is located on Gay Street. The Klotts Company built it, and it is the sister building to the more well-known and better-preserved facility in nearby Lonaconing. Here raw silk from the Orient was processed into thread, which was shipped to fabric weaving companies in Pennsylvania. The building sits vacant, but renovations are being made to transform it into condominiums. It is listed in the National Register of Historic Places. (Then image, courtesy of the A. Feldstein collection.)

The Kelly Springfield Tire Plant was built to produce truck tires in the years after World War I. It was a major employer in the region until 1987, when it closed after 66 years of operation. The county took over the riverside property and developed it as an industrial park. It now houses small- and medium-sized businesses and county offices. (Then image, courtesy of the A. Feldstein collection.)

The Queen City Brewery was located on Market Street between Wills Creek and the Western Maryland Railway tracks. The bottling house was located across Market Street, which is not visible in this photograph. A lot of the old brewery facility has been torn down, but a trucking firm uses some of the buildings, and the board of education uses the old bottling plant as a depot. (Then image by Vernon L. Penner, March 1975, courtesy of the A. Feldstein collection.)

The Wellington Glass Company was one of many glass manufacturing businesses in Cumberland. In this view, looking east, St. Patrick's Church and Carroll Hall are located in the upper left corner, and the Town Clock Church sits at the center top. Wellington Glass Company was formed in 1909 and used the property of the old Cumberland Glass Company, built in 1884. The factory burned in 1920 and was not rebuilt. (Then image, courtesy of the A. Feldstein collection.)

In 1871, the Baltimore and Ohio Railroad built the Rolling Mill Facility in Cumberland to recycle rail and other scrap steel into new railroad supplies. The railroad's Mount Clare Shops in Baltimore designed part of the complex, the Bolt and Forge Shop. The entire facility was demolished in 1981 and was replaced by a shopping center. The Rolling Mill Historic District includes some 173 properties, mostly 19th-century, working-class homes. (Then image, courtesy of the A. Feldstein collection.)

First National Bank,
Cumberland, Md.

The First National Bank Building is located at the corner of Baltimore and South George Streets. The building was constructed in 1912 and was designed by local architect Bruce Price. It was originally the Cumberland Bank of Allegany, founded 1812, and later became the First National Bank of Cumberland in 1864. Still operating as a financial institution, the building now houses the First Peoples Community Credit Union. (Then image, courtesy of the A. Feldstein collection.)

The Second National Bank in Cumberland
was chartered in 1865. This building, located
at Baltimore and South Liberty Streets, was
built in 1888. The architect, Bruce Price, also
designed the Emmanuel Episcopal Church
parish house, previously the Millholland
House, on Washington Street. The First
and Second National Banks merged in
1963 and occupied the Second National
Building. It currently hosts the Susquehanna
Bank. (Then image, courtesy of the A.
Feldstein collection.)

The Baltimore and Ohio Railroad Credit Union was organized to aid employees of the railroad in their financial and banking needs. The current Chessie Federal Credit Union at 141 Baltimore Street continues in that role and is open to all. The merger of the Baltimore and Ohio, the Chesapeake and Ohio, and the Seaboard Rail Systems, a direct predecessor to the current CSX Corporation, formed the Chessie system. The modern photograph shows the drive-up location. (Then image, courtesy of the M. McKenzie collection.)

The Third National Bank was charted in 1879 and occupied the building at Baltimore and Centre Streets in 1901. The Third National Bank merged with the Dime Savings bank, which then became the Liberty Trust Company. Now known as the Lila Building, the first floor housed the Allegany Museum through 2009. It was designed by local architect Wright Butler. The Cumberland and Westernport Electric Railway maintained a waiting room and express office in the building. (Then image, courtesy of the A. Feldstein collection.)

CHAPTER 4

GOVERNMENT

U. S. Post Office and Court House, Central Fire Department and Station House, Cumberland, Md.

Cumberland became the seat of Allegany County when it was formed from the westernmost part of Washington County. Thus it houses many city, county, and federal offices. Public services such as police and fire departments, municipal water, local transportation, the post office, National Guard units, the chamber of commerce, and others are represented. (Courtesy of the A. Feldstein collection.)

The neoclassical brick and stone Public Safety Building was built near the city hall at 19 Frederick Street in 1904. The building served as a federal courthouse, the sixth post office until 1930, a police station, the Health Department of Cumberland, and other city offices around 1934. It now houses a senior citizens center. It is on the National Register of Historic Places. (Then image, courtesy of the A. Feldstein collection.)

Originally, the Bell Tower Building was the Public Safety Building, housing the small Cumberland police force and the lock-up. Fire protection services were contracted out to independent companies. Then, the new Public Safety Building housed the city police. Now, a new public service building hosts both police and fire services and other city offices. The other buildings still stand. (Then image, courtesy of the A. Feldstein collection.)

The Cumberland Fire Department replaced independent hose companies that operated with a subscription service. Bringing the service under municipal jurisdiction standardized the service for all residents and businesses. In every age, firefighters are proud of their equipment. The photographs were taken roughly 100 years apart. (Then image, courtesy of the A. Feldstein collection; now image, courtesy of John A. Bone.)

GOVERNMENT

The modern city hall is about 100 years old and is listed on the National Register of Historic Places. It functions as the seat of the city government and is an architectural and historic site in its own right. It defines City Hall Plaza, which includes the Public Safety Building (fire and police departments) and the Bell Tower Building. (Then image, courtesy of the A. Feldstein collection.)

Bypass B
National
Cumberlar
U.

The bypass bridge on Henderson Boulevard provided a way for traffic to cross the busy west end of the Baltimore and Ohio Railroad tracks. It was built in 1932. It allows traffic to avoid a railroad grade crossing that had become a problem for fire trucks and ambulances to get to their north-end destinations when all crossings were blocked. (Then image, courtesy of the M. McKenzie collection.)

Originally the Company G Maryland National Guard Armory (1925–1960), this building now serves as the Cumberland Transportation Museum. The museum collection includes a recently restored Conestoga wagon. The facility was to be closed in July 2010 due to funding constraints, and the exhibits were to be placed in storage. Last-minute money was found to extend the life of the facility for another year. (Then image, courtesy of the A. Feldstein collection.)

The Allegany County Courthouse stands on Prospect Square and is an icon of the city's skyline. Local architect Wright Butler designed it, and it features gargoyles at the top of the tower. Built in 1893–1894, it is still in use as the courthouse and is the third building for that purpose since 1787. It is part of the Washington Street Historic District. It stands on the parade ground of Fort Cumberland. (Then image, courtesy of the A. Feldstein collection.)

The Allegany Public Library Main Branch stands on the site of a log courthouse built around 1840 and across the street from the current Allegany County Courthouse. The structure was built in 1849–1850 as the Allegany Academy. It is brick with Doric columns in the Greek Revival style and was built on the parade grounds of the original Fort Cumberland. By 1838, the Mechanics Circulating Library in Cumberland had acquired 300 volumes. The academy closed in 1929. (Then image, courtesy of the A. Feldstein collection.)

The Bell Tower Building in City Hall Plaza is a National Register property. It has served as the first Public Safety Building, the headquarters for the Allegany League for Crippled Children, the Cumberland Chamber of Commerce, and the police office and jail. It sits in City Hall Plaza, along with the new Public Service Building, which houses the police and fire departments. The building was long without a bell, but a new bell now resides in the tower. (Then image, courtesy of the A. Feldstein collection.)

The Post Office Building on Pershing Street replaced the post office facility in the second Public Safety Building on City Hall Square. This Post Office building later served a place for the district court, along with other offices. Currently, the building has been reopened as the home of the new Allegany County Museum. Shops and offices will also be located in the building. (Then image, courtesy of the A. Feldstein collection.)

The current post office occupies the site of the previous Baltimore and Ohio Railroad's Queen City Hotel and Station, located on the east side of the CSX tracks. It is conveniently located near the rails, but the trains no longer carry the mail. This post office replaced the one on Pershing Street, which became a district courthouse. (Then image, courtesy of the A. Feldstein collection; now image, courtesy of M. Stakem.)

The City Water Works at 72 Greene Street was pumping unfiltered water from the Potomac River and distributing it to the city by 1870. Unfortunately, due to upstream pollution, numerous epidemics swept through the population. Perhaps for the good of the public health, the waterworks burned down. A new city water supply was established in two artificial lakes in nearby Pennsylvania, and the incidences of infectious diseases like typhoid have been greatly reduced. (Then image, courtesy of the A. Feldstein collection; now image, courtesy of John A. Bone.)

PENNSYLVANIA
FISH & BOAT COMMISSION
GORDEN LAKE ACCESS
DEVELOPED FOR
PUBLIC FISHING & BOATING
IN COOPERATION WITH THE
CITY OF CUMBERLAND MARYLAND

The City Water Works at 72 Greene Street was a public health hazard but certainly aided firefighters. Mayor Thomas Koon was responsible for the new fresh water system. One of the lakes is, appropriately, Lake Koon. The site of the pump house is now a parking lot. (Then image, courtesy of the A. Feldstein collection.)

The Cumberland Fire Department of 1912 operated with state-of-the-art horse-drawn equipment. Today's department includes 65 firefighters and administrative and command personnel. The fire department has three stations with six pumper trucks, one aerial tower, one rescue truck, one command unit, and four advanced life support ambulances. The fire department began operations in 1906. The Central Fire Station is located at 20 Bedford Street. (Then image, courtesy of the A. Feldstein collection; now image, courtesy of John A. Bone.)

Fire Department, Cumberland, Md.

In the 1936 flood, Wills Creek again devastated downtown, another dramatic example of the need for the flood control project. The Army Corps of Engineers began studies for the project, which was delayed by World War II. The project was finally completed in the 1960s and has been successful to date in keeping the city dry. Wills Creek flows peacefully into the Potomac now. (Then image, courtesy of the M. McKenzie collection.)

This flood control construction scene from the 1950s was taken facing upstream from the Market Street Bridge. The Baltimore and Ohio Railroad viaduct is visible in the background crossing Wills Creek. The Queen City Brewery is to the left. Some mishap has swamped the crane in the creek bed. Today, the concrete walls tame Wills Creek, so it no longer floods the city. (Then image, courtesy of the M. McKenzie collection.)

In this view of the flood control construction, Wills Creek is visible. The low bridge in the background provided access for the Western Maryland Railway and is still in use by the Western Maryland Scenic Railway for access to its Ridgeley shops. Canal Place is to the left. The canal lock into the Potomac River has been covered by the flood control wall. (Then image, courtesy of the M. McKenzie collection.)

This scene shows the flood control construction in the area of the Market Street Bridge and the Queen City Brewery. The brewery used to dump untreated waste directly into Wills Creek, producing a yeasty smell and a "head" on the creek as far down as the confluence with Potomac. A trucking company now uses the brewery grounds, and the bottling house is used by the county school system. (Then image, courtesy of the M. McKenzie collection.)

These pictures were taken from the Baltimore Street Bridge over Wills Creek facing downstream. The Western Maryland Railway Station is to the left. The confluence of Wills Creek and the Potomac, coming from the right, can be seen. In the newer photograph, the Interstate 68 bridge and the new pedestrian bridge over Wills Creek can also be seen. (Then image, courtesy of the M. McKenzie collection.)

CHAPTER 5

TRANSPORTATION

In one small spot, the Baltimore and Ohio Railroad track alignment, Jefferson's National Road leading west, and the Chesapeake and Ohio Canal, which is now a national park that offers biking and hiking paths, can all be seen. The National Road was the first to be built, but the teamsters and stage drivers were pushed further west by the railroad. The canal hauled coal for many years but was devastated in a flood. (Courtesy of the M. McKenzie collection.)

The Western Maryland Railway freight warehouse was located behind the Western Maryland passenger station on Canal Street near the Times-New Building. The *Times-News* had its paper rolls delivered by rail. The rail siding for freight and the warehouse are gone, and the area is a parking lot and a press building. (Then image, courtesy of the M. McKenzie collection.)

Here is a watchman at the Western Maryland Railway crossing at Baltimore Street. Similarly today, when the Western Maryland Scenic Railway excursion train leaves for Frostburg, a brakeman from the train flags the crossing. The crossing guards' shack and safety gates are no longer in place. Trains have the right-of-way, even though most motorists seem to ignore that fact. (Then image, courtesy of the M. McKenzie collection; now image, courtesy of M. Stakem.)

The Western Maryland Railway Station was built in 1913. The last regularly scheduled passenger service ended in 1959. The station is on the National Register of Historic Places. The station and tracks are now used by the Western Maryland Scenic Railroad, which operates between Cumberland and Frostburg. In the modern photograph, recently restored locomotive No. 25 poses in the bright sun after a run to Frostburg. (Then image, courtesy of the M. McKenzie collection.)

The Western Maryland Railway Station currently serves as the Western Maryland Station Center, housing the ticket offices and gift shop for the Western Maryland Scenic Railroad, the National Park Service Office, a museum for the Chesapeake and Ohio Canal, and other small, private offices. A similar building now serves as the police department in Hagerstown, Maryland. (Then image, courtesy of the M. McKenzie collection.)

The Cumberland and Pennsylvania Railroad Bridge originally carried the 1840s Eckhart Branch Railroad across Wills Creek to merge with the Mount Savage Railroad, which ran into Cumberland. When the Baltimore and Ohio Railroad reached Cumberland in 1845, it found several local railroads ready to meet it. The four-arch brick structure stood until the 1990s, when it was removed to alleviate flooding upstream. (Then image, courtesy of the author.)

The Chesapeake and Ohio Canal, which built west from Georgetown near Washington, D.C., was designed to tap into the grain market of the Ohio River. Stalled at Cumberland for lack of funds, it hauled the region's coal exports. It is now a long and narrow national park, thanks to Supreme Court Justice William O. Douglas and others. The canal basin at Cumberland now houses the Shops at Canal Place and a motel. (Then image, courtesy of the M. McKenzie collection.)

The then-president of Baltimore and Ohio Railroad, John W. Garrett, built the Queen City Station and Hotel in 1872. The Italianate building cost $300,000 and had 150 guest rooms and a large ballroom. Currently, the Amtrak station occupies the site. Amtrak provides daily service between Washington and Pittsburgh through Cumberland. The demolition of the original structure in 1972 galvanized preservation and railroad history groups in the area. The building is listed on the National Register of Historic Places. (Then image, courtesy of the Nicholas Sullivan collection.)

The *Capitol Limited* was the Baltimore and Ohio Railroad's premier passenger train from New York, through Washington, D.C., to Chicago. Hauled originally by fast, streamlined steam engines, it converted to diesel engines in the 1940s. The B&O service ended in 1971. Today, Amtrak's *Capitol Limited* still runs through Cumberland. Every day two trains, one traveling eastbound and the other going westbound, use the CSX tracks. (Then image, courtesy of the M. McKenzie collection.)

The West Virginia Central and Pittsburgh Station, located at Baltimore Street and Wills Creek, served the railroad, which was eventually acquired by the Western Maryland Railroad. The site is now a park with murals of the early city. The Western Maryland Railway built a new passenger station nearby when rail service was completed to the east, connecting the Port of Baltimore with the West Virginia coalfields. (Then image, courtesy of the A. Feldstein collection.)

This view of the Hay Street passenger station at Viaduct Junction was taken looking south. In the modern photograph, both the Hay Street Station and the tower are gone, but the steeple of St. Patrick's Church gives the reference point. The station served the Cumberland and Pennsylvania Railroad and the Georges Creek and Cumberland Railroad. The B&O Queen City Station is just out of view down the tracks. (Then image, courtesy of the author.)

The Cumberland Road began in 1811 at a marker stone at lot No. 1 on Greene Street. The road traveled down Greene Street through Sandy Gap to Gwynn's Tavern (later the Six-Mile House) in LaVale. In 1835, the road was rerouted through the Narrows and joined the original route at Gwynn's. This project was initiated by President Jefferson, but maintenance was left to the states. The road east of Cumberland, leading to Baltimore, was privately funded. Now Interstate 68 passes over Cumberland. (Then image, courtesy of the A. Feldstein collection.)

The electric trolley system was first located within the city and later extended to outlying towns. It served the transportation needs of the expanding population. It allowed access to Cumberland from the outlying areas of the county. Now the Allegany County Transit buses, in tasteful colors, serve the same purpose. Transportation services to the new Allegany County Medical facility are particularly important. (Then image, courtesy of the author; now image, courtesy of John A. Bone.)

In the late 1890s, railroads hauled the long-distance freight, and express companies provided local delivery. This was before parcel service was introduced by the post office. The Baltimore and Ohio Railroad operated this horse and wagon. Today, packages reach their destinations by truck. (Then image, courtesy of the A. Feldstein collection; now image, courtesy of John A. Bone.)

In this scene near Greene Street, the Kneppers Pharmacy is visible. The location is now an optician's office. In the original photograph, a crew is clearing trees for the access for the new Blue Bridge (Route 28). This location is at Mile Post 1 on the National Road, which is marked with a memorial stone. (Then image, courtesy of the M. McKenzie collection.)

The Virginia Avenue underpass allows traffic to go under the busy lines of the Baltimore and Ohio Railroad. It is in use for pedestrians, vehicles, and livestock. The last cattle drive was in 1943. The herd moved from the Kline's Dairy in Wiley Ford, West Virginia. Livestock on the streets is probably now prohibited by city ordinance. (Then image, courtesy of the Dan Whetzel collection.)

CHAPTER 6

HOSPITALS AND CHURCHES

After the disastrous Braddock defeat, Fort Cumberland served as a troop hospital. During the Civil War, many facilities around the city were used as temporary hospital quarters. The area has a long tradition of solid medical care, culminating in the state-of-the-art facility just east of the city, which serves the entire county and region. (Courtesy of the A. Feldstein collection.)

Memorial Hospital was the successor to the Western Maryland Hospital and was owned and operated by the city. It served the community from 1929 until 2009. The new, modern Western Maryland Regional Medical Center complex consolidates health care for the region. The 275-bed facility opened in November 2009. Industrial and commercial tenants are now being sought for the old Memorial Building. (Then image, courtesy of the A. Feldstein collection.)

In 1888, the Western Maryland Hospital was built on Baltimore Avenue. The medical facilities were moved to the new Memorial Hospital in 1929. The building became the Allegany Inn, an 80-room hotel. Many people who stayed at the hotel considered it to be a spooky building. Some guest rooms, previously operating rooms, had blood drains in the floors. The building burned in 1973 under mysterious circumstances, and several people were killed. On the site now is a 10-story apartment building, the Cumberland Manor. (Then image, courtesy of the A. Feldstein collection.)

During the Civil War, a number of local buildings and churches were used as hospitals. One of these makeshift hospitals was the Clarysville Inn, which was sadly lost to fire in 1999. The Allegany Hospital on Decatur Street was organized around 1905. It was taken over by a Catholic organization in 1911 and became known as Sacred Heart Hospital in 1952. A new facility was built on Haystack Mountain in 1964, opening in 1967. The original site is now condominiums. (Then image, courtesy of the A. Feldstein collection.)

Allegany Hospital,
Cumberland, Md.

HOSPITALS AND CHURCHES

The new Sacred Heart Hospital was built by the Catholic Daughters of Charity on Haystack Mountain, west of Cumberland. The 240-bed facility opened in 1967. It was renamed the Western Maryland Health System Braddock Hospital. Now closed, it seeks a new use. In 2009, Memorial and Sacred Heart Hospitals were consolidated into the new Western Maryland Hospital System facility east of the city. (Then image, courtesy of the A. Feldstein collection.)

The German Catholic Monastery was founded by Westphalian Capuchin monks in 1875. It featured an imposing stone wall that enclosed the facility. It incorporated the earlier Church of SS. Peter and Paul. The monastery facility was self-sufficient in food. It included a training center for religious instruction. Adjacent to the facility is a school, a convent, and a parish house. (Then image, courtesy of the author.)

HOSPITALS AND CHURCHES

The Town Clock Church, at 312 Bedford Street, was built in 1848 by the German Lutherans. Two church towers were under construction that year, and the city agreed to provide a town clock to the one that finished first. It was a race, and the Lutherans worked around the clock to finish first. The property is listed on the National Register of Historic Places. (Then image, courtesy of the A. Feldstein collection.)

The Emmanuel Episcopal Church, a major icon of the Cumberland skyline, occupies the site of the original Fort Cumberland and has some of the original tunnels in its basement. The church grounds are decorated with Christmas trees during the holiday season. On Christmas Day in 1749, a Christian worship service took place at the site. Before Fort Cumberland was built, the site was used as a trading post for the Ohio Company. (Then image, courtesy of the A. Feldstein collection.)

HOSPITALS AND CHURCHES

CHAPTER 7

SCHOOLS AND PRIVATE HOMES

Many schools were and are located in Cumberland, ranging from kindergarten to Allegany College. Education has always been a priority for the area. From the mansions of Washington Street and the east side to the workers' town homes of Mechanic Street, all types of dwellings and styles are represented. (Then image, courtesy of the A. Feldstein collection.)

The Walsh House at 108 Washington Street has served as the headquarters for the Allegany County Board of Education since 1936. It was constructed in the 1860s in the Second Empire style. It was built by William Walsh, a lawyer and member of the House of Representatives. It is the birthplace of local missionary Bishop James Walsh, who was held prisoner by the Communist Chinese. The Washington Street Historic District includes six blocks of houses and mansions of the rich and famous. (Then image, courtesy of the Allegany Board of Education.)

SCHOOLS AND PRIVATE HOMES

J. P. Roman was president of the Second National Bank in Cumberland. His home, the Roman Mansion at 114 Washington Street, sat vacant for many years after his death. St. Paul's Lutheran Church was built on the site in 1958. The earlier St. Paul's Church on Baltimore Street had been torn down in 1957 to allow for commercial construction. (Then image, courtesy of the A. Feldstein collection, from *Artwork of Allegany County*, W. H. Parish Publishing, Chicago, 1897.)

The Dingle was an upscale gated development south and west of the city. It was a project of the Dingle Development Corporation in the early 1900s and was serviced by the Cumberland streetcar system. It is still a pleasant residential area of the city, although no longer gated. (Then image, courtesy of the A. Feldstein collection.)

SCHOOLS AND PRIVATE HOMES

History House, at 218 Washington Street, is maintained by the Allegany County Historical Society. Also know as the Gordon-Roberts House, it is listed on the National Register of Historic Places and is part of the Washington Street Historic District. Maintained by the historical society, it is decorated in period furnishings and accessories. The three-story building includes one bathroom, added later. (Then image, courtesy of the A. Feldstein collection.)

CARROLL CLUB, CUMBERLAND, MD.

Carroll Hall was built in 1903 as a social and sports center on North Centre Street. It was the meeting place of the Carroll Club and featured a stage for performances on the second floor. It became the LaSalle Institute, a high school for boys, from 1907 until 1966. The building was razed in 1987, and the site is now used as a parking lot for the nearby St. Patrick's Catholic Church. (Then image, courtesy of the A. Feldstein collection.)

SCHOOLS AND PRIVATE HOMES

The Masonic temple is located at 15 Greene Street and houses Potomac Masonic Lodge No. 100. It was chartered in 1855. Members used to meet at city hall, but when that burned down in 1910, the Masons decided to construct their own building for meetings. Wright Butler was the architect. It stands near the Emmanuel Episcopal Church on the grounds of Fort Cumberland. (Then image, courtesy of the A. Feldstein collection.)

asonic Temple, Cumberland, Md.

www.arcadiapublishing.com

Discover books about the town where you grew up, the cities where your friends and families live, the town where your parents met, or even that retirement spot you've been dreaming about. Our Web site provides history lovers with exclusive deals, advanced notification about new titles, e-mail alerts of author events, and much more.

MADE IN THE USA

Arcadia Publishing, the leading local history publisher in the United States, is committed to making history accessible and meaningful through publishing books that celebrate and preserve the heritage of America's people and places. Consistent with our mission to preserve history on a local level, this book was printed in South Carolina on American-made paper and manufactured entirely in the United States.

This book carries the accredited Forest Stewardship Council (FSC) label and is printed on 100 percent FSC-certified paper. Products carrying the FSC label are independently certified to assure consumers that they come from forests that are managed to meet the social, economic, and ecological needs of present and future generations.

FSC
Mixed Sources
Product group from well-managed forests and other controlled sources

Cert no. SW-COC-001530
www.fsc.org
© 1996 Forest Stewardship Council

Find Your Place in History.